CONTROVERSY ON THE CLYDE
ARCHAEOLOGISTS, FAKES AND FORGERS:
THE EXCAVATION OF DUMBUCK CRANNOG

Alex Hale and Rob Sands

Front cover:
'The Wild Boar Hunt at the Crannog'. William Donnelly's watercolour sketch, 1899. (SC687470)

Title page:
Donnelly's sketch of the excavations in progress on Dumbuck crannog. (SC709677)

Back cover:
An aerial photograph centred on the Dumbuck crannog, 2005. (SC970218)

ISBN 1-902419-45-6

© Crown Copyright:
RCAHMS 2005

Designed by Luise Valentiner
@ www.triggerpress.co.uk

Printed by Barr Printers
(Glenrothes) Ltd

TABLE OF CONTENTS

PREFACE

The interpretation of an antiquarian excavation is only as good as the archive that it produced. In the case of the Dumbuck crannog, excavated 1898-9, not only is the archive extensive, but it also contains a variety of media, which enables the interpretation to be detailed and well-illustrated. The title of this book refers to the controversy that developed as a result of the discovery of a small number of strange objects on the crannog, which did not fit easily with other known archaeological finds. These objects turned out to be forgeries, the work of an individual or more than one person who, for whatever reason, decided that the Dumbuck crannog should throw up much more than a well-preserved wooden structure.

Dumbuck crannog lies on the north shore of the Firth of Clyde, close to Dumbarton Rock. The surviving remains are partly covered by sands and silts, which provide a preservative environment for its oak piles, layers of brushwood and other delicate organic artefacts. Today, anybody walking past the crannog would find it difficult to believe that the forgeries discovered amongst the seaweed-covered stones and the odd stump of wood, could have caused such a lengthy debate. This debate was sometimes vitriolic, at times personal, and, most of all, carried out in public.

Today, we are fortunate that newscuttings, personal letters, photographs and glass lantern-slide copies of sketches from the original excavator's notebooks survive and are held at the Royal Commission on the Ancient and Historical Monuments of Scotland (RCAHMS). What follows is the story of the Dumbuck crannog, as told through the RCAHMS archive. It also draws upon the archives and objects held in other institutions, and shows how they fit into the history of the site and the controversy.

The contents of the RCAHMS archive, which contains information on all aspects of the built heritage of Scotland, can be accessed in person at the Public Search Room, RCAHMS, John Sinclair House, 16 Bernard Terrace, Edinburgh, EH8 9NX. Enquiries may also be made by telephone: 0131-662 1456, or fax: 0131-662 1477/1499. Alternatively, the RCAHMS Canmore database can be searched on line at www.rcahms.gov.uk, and many images are now available on line. All illustrations in this book are Crown Copyright: RCAHMS, unless otherwise stated. The RCAHMS images are accompanied by their relevant catalogue number. Other images used are copyright Sands and Hale or they are accompanied by the relevant copyright credit. The location map is based on an Ordnance Survey map with the permission of Ordnance Survey on behalf of the Controller of Her Majesty's Stationary Office © Crown Copyright. All rights reserved. OS Licence number 100020548 2005.

The authors have collaborated on researching Dumbuck and the other crannogs in the Firth of Clyde since 1998. Alex Hale is an Archaeological Investigator at RCAHMS and Rob Sands is the Information Technology and Computing Specialist at UCD School of Archaeology. The authors would like to acknowledge the help and assistance of the following: Claire Brockley, Dave Cowley, Tahra Duncan, Lesley Ferguson, Iain Fraser, Strat Halliday, James Hepher, Alan Leith, Jack Stevenson and Kristina Watson of RCAHMS; UCD School of Archaeology; Historic Scotland for funding the excavations on Dumbuck, 2000-1; Andrea Smith, Director of the Society of Antiquaries of Scotland for allowing us to reproduce the image of Joseph Anderson; Graham Hopner, Dumbarton Public Library; Douglas Hoad at Clydeport; Anya Clayworth; Angela McAteer; the members of ACFA who helped erect the photographic tower in 1998; Rob Shaw, the Discovery Programme and Shona Corner, Valerie Hunter and Helen Smailes, National Galleries of Scotland for figure 4. The glass lantern-slides were deposited with RCAHMS as a result of the diligence of the late Dr J N Graham Ritchie, to whom the authors are most grateful.

INTRODUCTION

This book tells the story of a forgotten archaeological controversy which smouldered for over 30 years after the excavation of the Dumbuck crannog in 1898-9. The controversy was triggered by a number of forgeries, which came to be known as the 'queer things' from the Clyde. Dumbuck lies in the intertidal zone on the north shore of the Firth of Clyde, between Dumbarton Rock and Bowling Harbour (NS 4167 7392). The site today, as then, is exposed only at low tide, and comprises a circular timber platform.

Over the past 35 years a substantial archive of original notes, personal communications, press cuttings, published articles, photographs, books and glass lantern-slides, has been deposited with RCAHMS. This book presents the principal figures, reconstructs the key sequence of excavations and events, theorizes about the likely perpetrators of the forgeries, and brings the story of Dumbuck crannog up to date with an outline of current research. The book also attempts to paint a picture of a 19th-century excavation, for Dumbuck is unique in having been recorded in a series of watercolours and character sketches by William A Donnelly, an artist of national repute and a local to the Dumbarton area. Donnelly produced sketches and watercolours of work in progress during 1898-9 and was instrumental in both instigating and directing the excavations on the site. The location of his sketchbooks is currently unknown. Fortunately, however, many of the original paintings were recorded onto glass lantern-slides, which now form part of the J Harrison Maxwell Collection, held by RCAHMS.

Today, Dumbuck crannog lies on the shores of a canalised river, backed by saltmarsh, which is hemmed in by a railway line (see back cover). It is rarely visited by people walking along the shore of the Firth of Clyde and remains almost forgotten. The controversy too has long since passed. But modern techniques and changes in archaeological thought have moved on, enabling fresh perspectives to be brought to bear and new information to be derived from the crannog and the archive. In this respect, Dumbuck still has much more to offer.

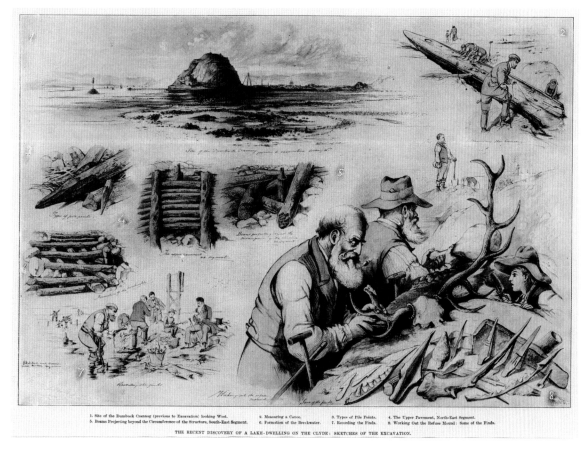

Fig. 1 'The Recent Discovery of a Lake-Dwelling on the Clyde. Sketches of the Excavation'. One of Donnelly's composite sketches published in the Illustrated London News, *8 October 1898. (SC936015)*

Recent archaeological research has revealed that there are at least three other similar sites in the Firth of Clyde (Fig. 7) and another group in the Beauly Firth, near Inverness (Hale 2004). With this greater corpus of marine crannogs has come a broader understanding of their age, form and function. Part of Dumbuck has recently been dated using radiocarbon methods and the results place the construction phase of the timber platform to between the 2nd century BC and the 2nd century AD. This corresponds closely with dates from one of the other crannogs in the Clyde, situated upstream near Erskine Bridge (Sands and Hale 2001, 48), and with those from a logboat found in the same area (Mowat 1996, 129). This cluster of dates suggests a lively and well-used river and shoreline.

Archaeological surveys of other marine crannogs have revealed a range of structural remains surviving in the intertidal mud (Hale 2000). They include timber platforms comparable to that at Dumbuck, although they vary in shape and in size. Unlike freshwater crannogs, the marine sites appear to be built directly onto old land surfaces, which suggests that they were dry when constructed and have since been flooded by local changes in the tidal range. Surveys of the surrounding mudflats have identified that the sites form raised mounds in an otherwise level foreshore, and they are positioned on the ends of low promontories jutting out into the water. This choice of position must have been deliberate, perhaps in order to allow access to and from the river.

While archaeology has moved on and techniques have developed, it is salutary to observe that in many senses some of the core questions raised by the 19th-century excavators remain. Our ability to systematically record archaeological information has developed, we have a much better understanding of the sediments, we can reconstruct the environment with a degree of accuracy hitherto unobtainable, and our ability to date sites, especially ones with good organic survival, is unsurpassed. However, even today,

we can still ask what is a crannog? and not expect to have a single answer or one upon which all agree. Many structures have been referred to as crannogs, mainly in Scotland (Morrison 1985) and Ireland (O'Sullivan 1998). What is clear is that the term crannog has been used to label an array of structures of differing dates, in differing localities, and probably of differing function. The connecting factor between these structures is merely that they are wholly or partly artificial, and are located on or very close to a water body. Comparatively few have been looked at in detail, but research continues. What shines through, is that each of these structures has a remarkable and individual story (Crone 2000).

THE DUMBUCK ARCHIVE

Given the location of the crannog, one might expect the majority of the archive and objects to be found in the west of the country. To a certain extent this is the case, and there is Dumbuck material in Glasgow, Dumbarton and Helensburgh. Glasgow City Archive, at the Mitchell Library, contains a plan of Dumbuck, which appears to have come from one of Donnelly's sketchbooks. The Glasgow Art Gallery and Museum, at Kelvingrove, holds the wooden ladder and the conserved remains of the logboat. The majority of the small finds, which are central to the controversy, however, are in the National Museum of Scotland. The material held at RCAHMS has been deposited over the past 35 years. It can be divided into three parts: a paper archive collected at the time of the excavation and during the ensuing controversy by Ludovic M Mann; glass lantern-slides from the J Harrison Maxwell collection; and aerial photographs taken since the 1940s.

Ludovic Mann (1869-1955), an accountant and insurance broker by profession, was an avid collector of artefacts and actively promoted archaeology through exhibitions, articles in newspapers and the radio (Ritchie 2002). During his lifetime, he amassed an extensive collection of notes, photographs, correspondence, lectures, drawings and newscuttings covering a wide range of archaeological sites, discoveries and interpretations. A significant amount of the information about Dumbuck has come from this collection, bequeathed by Mann to George Applebey and subsequently gifted to RCAHMS in 1990.

J Harrison Maxwell (d.1971) also undertook archaeological research and excavations on a number of sites and was guided in his work by Mann, referring in the publication report on the Bronze Age cemetery at Springhill Farm, Baillieston, near Glasgow, to his *'friend, guide, critic and master, Mr Ludovic McLellan Mann'* (Maxwell 1939). Maxwell lectured to Adult Education classes and illustrated his talks with glass lantern-slides, including colour copies of the Dumbuck drawings. When Maxwell died in 1971, his collection was deposited in RCAHMS.

When Donnelly's sketches were photographed, or whether it was indeed Mann or Maxwell who arranged for the copying, is not known. Mann certainly knew Donnelly and visited the excavations at Dumbuck, noting in a lecture in 1932 how he had found a bone amulet under the logboat (RCAHMS, MS/678/192).

Fig. 2 A photograph of Donnelly, posing with sketchbook in hand and some of the Dumbuck small finds to his left. (SC960811)

WILLIAM DONNELLY:
ARTIST AND ARCHAEOLOGIST

Central to understanding the events that took place at Dumbuck are William Donnelly's pictures, reproduced on the glass lantern-slides. These enduring images reveal Dumbuck through Donnelly's eyes, together with a cast of characters that appear in letters and press cuttings as the controversy unfolds. Donnelly was born in 1847, son of William and Elizabeth Donnelly, and at the time of the 1881 census was living in Woodside Cottage, Old Kilpatrick, Dumbarton. He married Helen Haggart, from Fife, on 11 May 1885, and they had three children: William Gerald (b.1885); Francis (b.1889); and Helen (b.1895).

William Donnelly: artist
Donnelly's pursuit of an artistic career is perhaps unsurprising, given his family background. His great-grandfather, William Gerald Donnelly, had co-founded a printworks, Donnelly and Shuttleworth, based in Cork in 1810, and his grandfather was also in the print business. His father was a pattern designer, co-founding his own company, Donnelly and Ralston of Buchanan Street, Glasgow. This artistic pedigree clearly rubbed off on both William and his sisters, who are all referred to as artists in the 1881 census. Donnelly's career was both prolific and well-regarded. Nationally he was perhaps best known for his work in the popular newspaper, the *Illustrated London News*, for which he acted as the Scottish correspondent. Notably, he was one of the first people on the scene of the now infamous Tay Bridge disaster, and recorded the event for the London paper. His artistic works and journalistic connections brought him to the attention of several influential figures of his day, such as Lord Overtoun, and also resulted in personal commissions from the Royal Family.

Donnelly's surviving painted and drawn work illustrates not only his skill and ability, but also the breadth of his subjects. This small corpus of work comprises ten pictures and provides a fascinating insight into royalty, civic events, landscapes of the Clyde and town scenes in the west of the country at the turn of the century. The relatively small number of paintings suggests that there are more in private collections, which may include examples unattributed to Donnelly. West Dumbartonshire Council Fine Art Collection holds four paintings and a print attributed to Donnelly. The paintings comprise an imposing image of Lord Overtoun addressing an audience at the *'Corn Exchange'*, two images of Dumbowie dun during excavations, and a watercolour landscape of the north bank of the Clyde looking towards Dumbarton Rock. The print shows the opening of Dumbarton Pier in

Fig. 3 *A photograph of Donnelly, probably with his son Gerald, once again with sketchbook in hand. (SC709729)*

1875, and Donnelly features as a member of the crowd on the ship moored at the end of the pier. This cameo role recurs in his paintings and the Dumbuck sketches. One of the other five paintings shows the interior of St Patrick's Church, Dumbarton. Another painting depicts Dumbarton in an early evening view looking south down Church Street past the Burgh buildings, with the spire of Riverside Parish Church in the background. Another of Donnelly's paintings of a civic event is entitled *'The laying of the foundation stone of the new post office, George Square'*. This was undertaken by HRH the Prince of Wales on 17 October 1876. The remaining two pictures are fine watercolours, one of which shows *'Dunters'* public house at Littlemill, Bowling, and the other, Dumbarton Rock and a shipyard.

Fig. 4 'The Leven Shipyard, on the Clyde, Dumbarton'. Executed by Donnelly over almost thirty years (1865-93).
(Reproduced with kind permission of the National Galleries of Scotland. Copyright: The Scottish National Portrait Gallery)

The second of these watercolours was recently purchased by the National Galleries of Scotland (Fig. 4). The image was executed from Castle Street, Dumbarton, where the road bridges the canalised mouth of the Knowle Burn. Beneath Dumbarton Rock is the site of Denny and Rankin's Shipyard, which became Denny's Leven yard around 1870, beyond is the Firth of Clyde. Donnelly features in the foreground of this painting, standing on Castle Street with his back to the viewer. Throughout the Dumbuck excavations Donnelly used his artistic skills to document the proceedings. He is seen on site in at least two photographs with sketchbook in hand. Tell-tale creases in one or two of the surviving images suggests they were done in a sketchbook whilst he was on the crannog (Fig. 5).

William Donnelly: archaeologist

In addition to his artistic endeavours, Donnelly had two other great passions, ornithology and archaeology, and he was a regular and prominent member of The Helensburgh Naturalist and Antiquarian Society (to be referred to hereafter as the Helensburgh Society). Donnelly only undertook active archaeological investigations relatively late in life. Nevertheless, under the auspices of the Helensburgh Society he collaborated on the excavation of four sites: Sheep Hill, Auchentorlie (1894); Dumbowie (1895); Dumbuck (1898) and Auchengaich (1900). However, despite his late start, in 1894 he was awarded life membership of the British Antiquarian Association of London in recognition of his archaeological work around Dumbarton.

Sheep Hill, Auchentorlie fort
(Canmore number NS47SW 6)
Donnelly worked with John Bruce in 1894 investigating the fort at Auchentorlie, usually referred to today as Sheep Hill, during which time they recorded and identified a number of rocks carved with cup and cup-and-ring markings (Bruce 1896, 205-9). Donnelly contributed two illustrations to the paper, showing the carvings at Auchentorlie and Conchno (Bruce 1896, Plates V and VI). Towards the left hand side of Plate V there are two small vignettes, one showing the general location of the carved panel, the other depicts a carved boulder. Filling the page with vignettes in this way seems to be a recurring style that Donnelly adopted and later used to illustrate Dumbuck.

Dumbowie dun
(Canmore number NS47NW 1)
Donnelly played an important part in the identification and excavations of Dumbowie dun in 1895. Like Dumbuck, the site was brought to the attention of the Helensburgh Society by Donnelly, and the excavations were undertaken by one of the then Secretaries, Adam Millar. Millar's report includes a pen-and-ink drawing of the excavated dun by Donnelly (Millar 1896, Fig. 1). Donnelly also produced the two oil paintings of the dun now held by West Dumbartonshire Council. The paintings show the dun from the north, with Dumbarton Rock and Castle in the background, and the Firth of Clyde running across the canvas. They were painted to illustrate different stages of the excavation. One shows the interior partially excavated, with the inner face of the enclosing wall exposed and the outer face still grass-grown. The other shows the wall free-standing, with the outer face exposed and the interior more extensively cleared. Like Dumbuck, the Dumbowie excavations were partly overshadowed by some unusual finds. They included arrow-shaped slate objects with incised lines and small slabs of rock marked by holes and curvilinear lines. These objects are almost certainly by the same hand that made those found on Dumbuck and have also been dismissed as forgeries (Munro 1905).

Auchengaich shieling-huts
(Canmore number NS29SE 1)
In September 1900 Donnelly investigated two of the large group of shieling-huts and mounds scattered between tributaries of the Auchengaich Burn. He subsequently

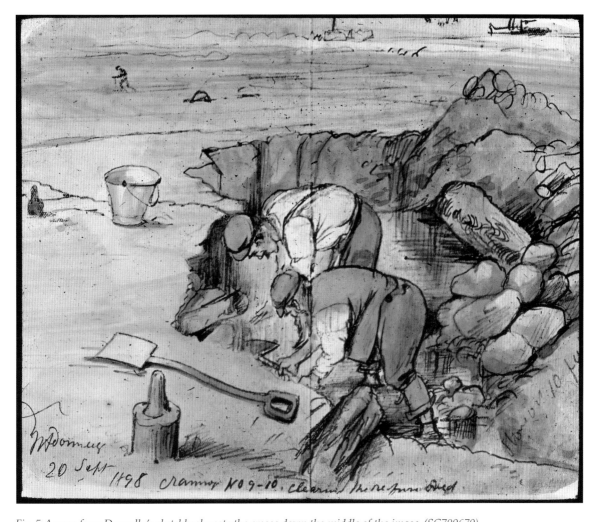

Fig. 5 A page from Donnelly's sketchbook: note the crease down the middle of the image. (SC709679)

published four articles on his findings, which were illustrated with his characteristic vignettes, and included himself and the other excavators in the pictures (Donnelly 1900). This appears to be the last archaeological site that Donnelly investigated.

DUMBUCK CRANNOG:
A 19TH-CENTURY EXCAVATION

Dumbuck crannog is located on the Firth of Clyde, a short distance to the east of Dumbarton Rock and Castle (Fig. 7). Occasionally, crannogs occur in estuaries around the coast of Scotland, and Dumbuck is one of four known examples in the inner Firth of Clyde. Dumbuck is exposed only on a falling tide and the visible remains comprise a circular wooden platform within a ring of upright posts, all enclosed by a stone and timber breakwater. Recent research shows that it dates to between the 2nd century BC and the 2nd century AD and suggests that it was built as a water-side platform rather than a dwelling (Hale 2004). Changes to the channel of the River Clyde, especially following the introduction of dredging and the construction of training walls in the 19th century, have contributed to its subsequent submergence. The diurnal flooding by the tides and the wet estuarine silts have ensured the continued preservation of the timbers and other organic remains of this remarkable site.

Fig. 6 Work at Dumbuck crannog in 1898, with Dumbarton Rock and Castle in the background. (SC709695)

The discovery: July 1898

It was William Donnelly's enthusiasm for archaeology that led to the discovery of Dumbuck crannog on Sunday, 31 July 1898. As a member of the Helensburgh Society, Donnelly had both found and helped to direct the investigation of the dun site at Dumbowie.

The Dumbowie excavation and other discoveries in the area had led Donnelly to the conclusion *'that other evidence of his* [prehistoric man's] *presence might, or rather should, be found nearer the great river itself'* (1898a, 283). It was this conviction that led him to take regular walks along the banks of

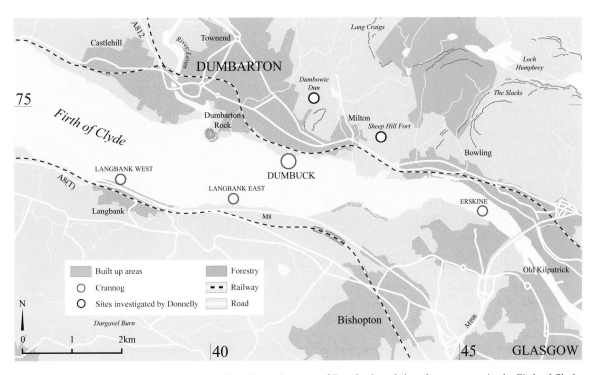

Fig. 7 Location map of Dumbuck and the other crannogs in the Firth of Clyde.

the river and, on that Sunday afternoon in July, he noticed timbers protruding from the foreshore silts. Closer examination revealed the remains of a wooden platform surrounded by 27 posts in a near perfect circle, which gave all the indications of being a substantial and unique structure.

Donnelly wasted no time in drawing the site to the attention of Dr Joseph Anderson, Keeper of the National Museum of Antiquities of Scotland and also Assistant Secretary of the Society of Antiquaries of Scotland. Anderson in his turn informed Dr Robert Munro MD, the authority on

Fig. 8 'Site of the Dumbuck Crannog. And the Country Around Looking North', 1899. (SC709661)

crannogs at the time and the Honorary Secretary of the Society of Antiquaries of Scotland.

Munro first visited the site on Tuesday, 16 August 1898 and as Donnelly records:

'The Doctor at the first glance was convinced that a dwelling was there, and at once commenced to prove it, by making at least half a dozen small excavations, which earned for my find his opinion that "it was the most curious, puzzling, and interesting find of the kind he had met in all his long experience". He added that no time should be lost in having it thoroughly and carefully excavated, great care being taken in sifting the refuse mound, and further pointed out the great value evidence of fire or habitation would attach to the find.' (Donnelly 1898a, 283)

Spurred on by Munro's comments, Donnelly encouraged the excavation committee of the Helensburgh Society to visit the site later that August. During this visit:

Fig. 9 Dr Joseph Anderson. (Reproduced by kind permission of the Society of Antiquaries of Scotland)

'*Another attack was made on the dwelling: this time, although slight, of a more practical kind; resulting in revealing the fact that there was design and execution in the building, occupation, habitation (over a lengthened period), positive evidence of fire, and splendid evidence of life at the period. This was proved by the fact of the presence of large quantities of the bones of stag, cow, horse, sheep, and other smaller animals, besides quantities of shells, from which shell fish had been taken after being roasted. The positive evidence of the use of fire was visible in fragments of calcined bones and charcoal, besides a number of fire-stones. A flint arrowhead, and a very fine hone, or sharpener was also found, the latter of fine ground sandstone.*' (Donnelly 1898a, 283-4)

Following this visit an extraordinary meeting of the Helensburgh Society was called in order to decide how to proceed. Donnelly had already determined in his own mind that an excavation was required, and fortunately the rest of the committee were of like mind and '*were willing that the Dumbowie efforts should be repeated*' (Donnelly 1898a, 284).

Fig. 10 Dr Robert Munro M D (after Morrison 1985)

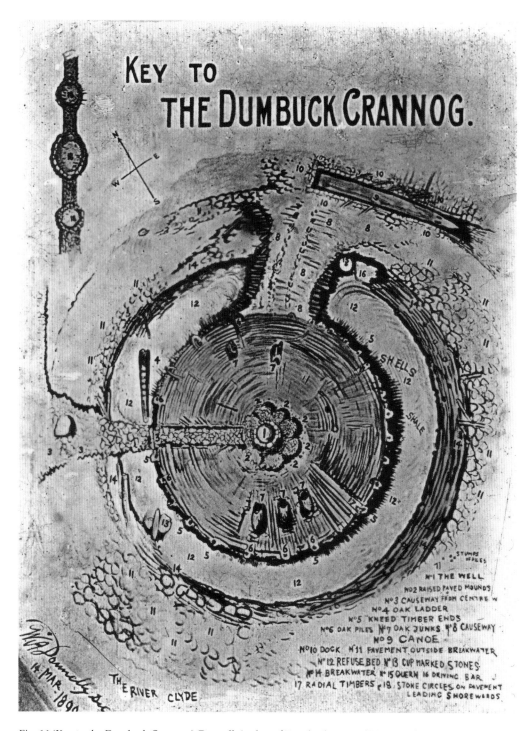

Fig. 11 'Key to the Dumbuck Crannog', Donnelly's plan of Dumbuck, 1899. (SC709671)

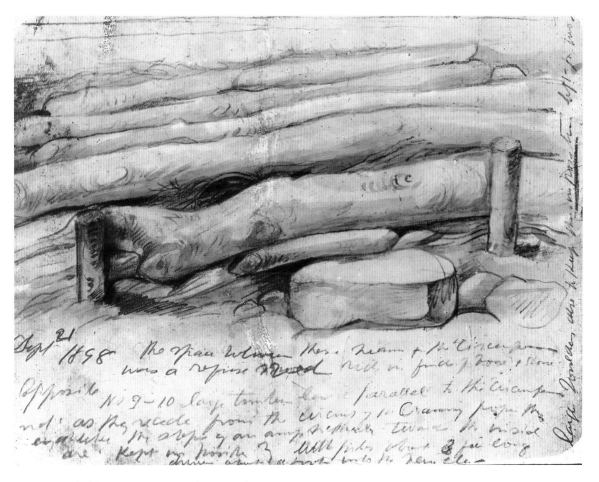

Fig. 12 Detail of the breakwater, 1898. (SC709687)

The structure of the crannog

As seen through Donnelly's eyes the plan of the crannog was a circular platform, within and around which there were several distinct features (Fig. 11). At its very heart was a 1.8m wide wattle- and clay-lined pit surrounded by up to seven small mounds of stones, each of which were encircled by wooden piles. These features are difficult to detect when one visits the site today. The pit lay at the centre of a wooden platform, which was made up of layers of roundwood, laid both radially and tangengentially. Donnelly identified three distinct layers of wood, underlain by brushwood and in its turn, stones, and the whole edifice rested on blue clay. The platform was contained within a ring of 27 relatively evenly-spaced oak piles, surrounded by a feature described by Donnelly and his co-workers as *'the refuse bed'*.

Fig. 13 The causeway that runs from the platform towards the Witches Plantain Burn. (SC709696)

Fig. 14 The path leading from the platform to the boat dock. (SC709692)

Outside of the refuse bed there was a ring of brushwood described as a breakwater, consisting of *'nine rows of timbers, jammed and held in place by softwood piles'* (Donnelly 1898b, 373). On the sketch of this feature, Donnelly adds that the structure is laid out as if in steps, retained in place by little piles, about 0.9m long, driven about 0.3m into the blue clay (Fig. 12). Beyond the breakwater Donnelly describes a *'pavement'* 6.9m wide running around the whole circuit of the site, laid *'like a rough causewayed farmyard'* and constructed from different kinds of stone. The brushwood breakwater and the pavement, presumably a stone breakwater, are not obvious when one visits the site today. These features were probably altered during excavation and as a result of subsequent activity. For example, stones have clearly been moved around to create a duck-shooting hide on one part of the site.

Leading from the platform Donnelly records two pathways, one a stone causeway leading to the west, and the other a wooden path to the north-east, leading towards a wooden shuttered logboat dock some 1.2m deep. The causeway ended at a line of stones, which ran directly inland along the eastern edge of an artificial channel known at the time as Witches Plantain Burn (Fig. 13). It was conjectured at the time that these stones were originally derived from Dumbuck. The burn no longer follows this course having breached the line of stones close to the edge of the salt marsh, and its course now curves around the east side of the crannog.

Fig. 15 The logboat and dock under excavation. (SC676473)

Other key features that are also mentioned or illustrated include some larger timbers, which sat on or were embedded in the platform (Fig. 17). These are still visible today, although it is hard to determine the accuracy of the description given by Bruce, who also published a detailed account of the excavations:

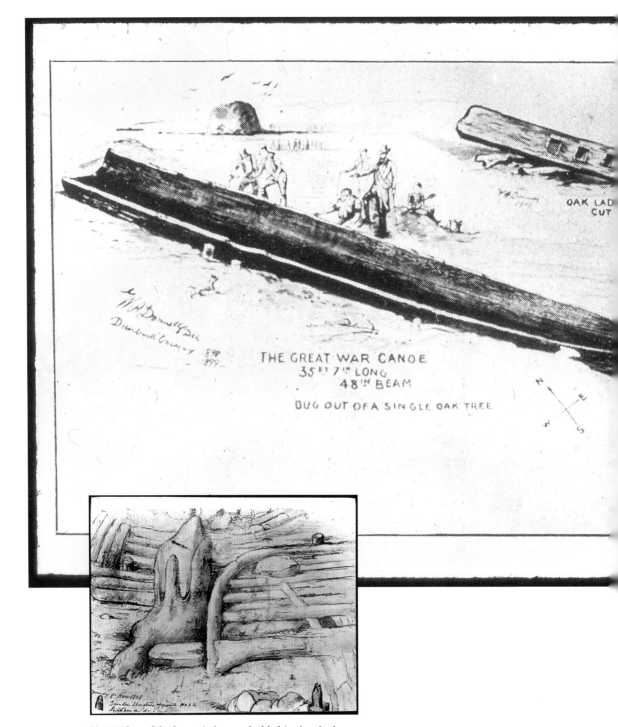

THE GREAT WAR CANOE
35 FT 7 IN LONG
48 IN BEAM

DUG OUT OF A SINGLE OAK TREE

Fig. 17 One of the large timbers embedded in the platform, 1898. (SC709694)

Labels within the image:
PATHWAY
CAUSEWAY TIMBER & BOULDERS
QUERN
INGLE OAK PLANK
BOULDERS
TYPES OF STONE FINDS
FROM DUMBUCK CRANNOG

Fig. 16 The logboat, dock and a collection of small finds. (SC709708)

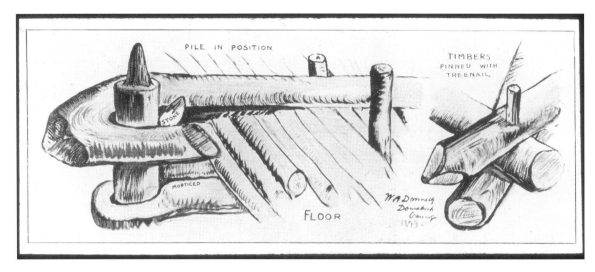

Fig. 18 Construction details of the platform, 1898. (SC709713)

'Midway between the centre and the outside piles of the structure what looked at first to be tree roots or snags were noticed partly imbedded in the sand. On being washed of the adhering soil, holes of 12 inches [0.3m] wide by 25 inches [0.6m] deep were found cut in them at an angle, to all appearance for the insertion of struts for the support of an upper structure. On the outside, 14 inches [0.35m] down on either side, holes of 2 inches [5cm] diameter were found intersecting the central hole, apparently for the insertion of a wooden key or treenail to retain the strut.'
(Bruce 1900, 438)

In this article Bruce reveals further details of the construction, many of which were also captured in Donnelly's sketches (Fig. 18).

'At all the piles a larger tree than those forming the flooring proper has been used, either with the natural knee or fork, or a similar recess mortised to fit the pile; and to make the locking more secure, stone wedges or jams have been used.'
(Bruce 1900, 437)

Donnelly made some attempt to capture the basic stratigraphy of the sediments upon which the platform stood, revealed by the removal of two of the piles during excavation, and later by a cut section (Fig. 19).

Note that his drawing of the pile assumes that the pointed upper end was a design feature when in fact this is the way that exposed oak naturally erodes, the harder heart wood surviving for longer than the outer surface.

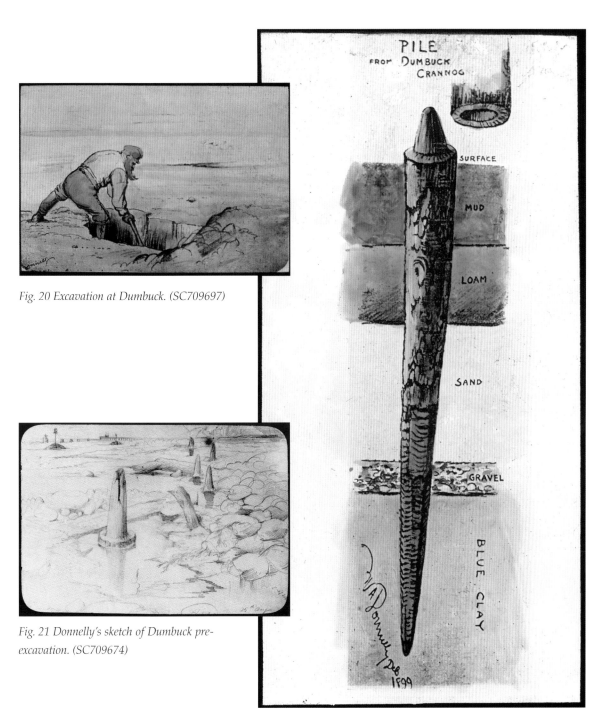

Fig. 20 Excavation at Dumbuck. (SC709697)

Fig. 21 Donnelly's sketch of Dumbuck pre-excavation. (SC709674)

Fig. 19 'Pile from Dumbuck Crannog'. Donnelly's schematic section, 1899. (SC709711)

Fig. 22 John Bruce (by bucket) and William Donnelly (right) excavating at Dumbuck crannog in 1898. (SC709728)

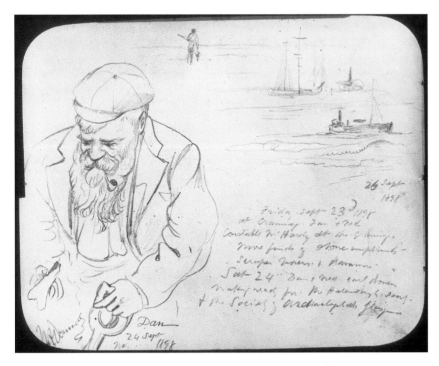

Fig. 23 Dan contemplating a recent find, 1898. (SC709691)

Excavation 1898-1899

Nineteenth-century excavation clearly lacked many of the techniques and procedures that we take for granted today. While most of the key principles had been established by the late 1800s, the actual practice of archaeology was mostly conducted by amateur groups with a variable range of knowledge and skills.

The excavation of Dumbuck also came at a time when there was a growing interest in crannog studies. In 1866, John Stuart published the first list of crannogs in Scotland (Stuart 1866), and subsequently Robert Munro undertook extensive researches into Scottish and European lake dwellings (Munro 1882, 1890). Similar scholarly interest had been generated in Ireland in the 1800s, culminating in the publication of William Wood-Martin's book in 1886. In Scotland Munro undertook a series of excavations, mainly in the south-west of the country, which formed the beginnings of modern crannog studies. He was followed in the first decade of the 20th century, by Father Odo Blundell (Blundell 1909). Blundell's work concentrated in Highland lochs and he was probably the first Scottish underwater archaeologist. It was Munro's expertise that was called upon in the first instance to confirm the veracity of the crannog at Dumbuck.

Fig. 24 Ned (left) and Dan (right) returning after a digging session. (SC709703)

Fig. 25 'Home from Doing the Crannog', 1898. (SC709706)

It was a relatively experienced group who embarked on the investigation of Dumbuck. Nevertheless, it is important to realise that the task they set themselves was not an easy one, and that they had no experience of excavating crannogs. Riverine mud and silt, combined with tidal flooding, makes any excavation difficult to manage with any degree of finesse. Excavation at Dumbuck commenced in August 1898 under the auspices of the excavation committee of the Helensburgh Society. Three members of the committee, John Bruce, William Donnelly and Adam Millar, directed the excavation, and the whole endeavour was financed by the Society.

Fig. 26 'The Inrushing Tide Hunts Ned and Dan', 1898. (SC709678)

Throughout the excavation Donnelly was at pains to make daily notes and sketches, many of which he used as the basis of his illustrations that accompanied his articles in the local press and in the *Illustrated London News*. Donnelly evidently wanted to advertise and promote the excavations to a broad an audience as possible. It is clear from these numerous illustrations and newspaper articles that work progressed at the crannog through a combination of local volunteers, members of the Helensburgh Society and hired hands (RCAHMS, MS/678/35). Three hired workers

are referred to by Bruce in a letter to the *Glasgow Herald* dated 10 February 1899, though the first names of only two of the workers are known: Ned and Dan. Both figure consistently in Donnelly's sketches (Figs 23 and 24).

While Ned and Dan formed the core work force, members of the Helensburgh Society made regular contributions, and the excavation was clearly seen as a place where the general public could come along for a little bit of recreational digging. In one image we see a young lad, probably accompanied by his

Fig. 27 A flooded trench on the edge of the crannog, 1898. (SC709688)

mother and sisters, heading home after a day out excavating on the crannog (Fig. 25).

Progress was initially reported through the pages of the *Journal of the British Archaeological Association*. Working at Dumbuck required careful timing in order to avoid the incoming tide. On an average day there would have been approximately 3-4 hours of exposure either side of a low tide, which in reality would have given a working time of no more than 6 hours. Clearly the tide sometimes caught the excavators on the hop (Fig. 26).

Not only did the excavators have to contend with the tides, they also found their excavations continually filled up with water as they dug deeper. These problems and the solution was mentioned on more than one occasion:

'A great difficulty which has to be contended with is the tide. To cope with this, and to enable work to be carried on, deep ducts have had to be cut in tangent form in order to drain away the water which continually collects when excavations are made.' (*Evening Times*, 14 October 1898)

Fig. 28 Excavation of the central pit. (SC691876)

Articles in the press and Donnelly's sketches of the excavation in progress, make it clear that the excavators' main focus was what they referred to as the refuse bed. They dug along this feature in a technique reminiscent of the 'wall-chasing' of many earlier 19th-century excavations, which involved following the line of a wall:

'My own feeling in regard to this discovery is to make a thorough excavation and examination of every handful of earth or debris in and near to at least 12ft. [3.6m] outside the piles; for, indeed, I have verified the refuse mound to extend 12ft. outside for a great part of the circuit, rich in finds of various kinds: so that I feel strongly that every spadeful of the area I name should be sifted.' (Donnelly 1898a, 285)

The refuse bed was not the only feature to be examined, and excavations were also conducted within some of the more obvious structures, such as the central wattle-lined pit and the boat dock, both of which were excavated to their base. The excavation of the central pit began sometime on, or shortly after, 31 October 1898 (Fig. 28). Donnelly describes its uncovering and subsequent excavation:

Fig. 29 Ned uncovering the path to the boat dock. (SC709693)

'The boulders, when bared, gradually disclosed a perfect circle. The circle of stones enclosed a cavity the sides of which were lined round and round, as well as bottom, with hazel wattles, which had been plaited while pliable and green; afterwards the cavity had been systematically puddled with superior quality of blue-till well kneaded in. The hazel bark is as clear and beautiful as the day it was cut, but the interior fibre is perfect pulp.'
(Donnelly 1898b, 372)

Throughout the excavation wooden structures and a series of finds were uncovered and removed from the site. While most of these finds were small and easily dealt with, others were larger, such as a possible ladder, two of the twenty-seven piles and the logboat found in the dock (Figs 30 and 31). The ladder caused much conjecture amongst the excavators and contributed to the public debate concerning the form of the site. For some it implied a structure with a raised or second floor.

Fig. 30 The excavation of the ladder, 1898. (SC709690)

The logboat was some 12.3m in length and cut from a single trunk of oak. The excavation and removal of this item required a large labour force and the cooperation of the Clyde Trust.

'The dispersing mists and darkness of Friday morning on the Clyde revealed the presence at the crannog of a Clyde Trust tug, three punts, and a staff of over thirty men, dispatched by Mr Deas, with all appliances and equipment, for the excavation and safe removal of the great war canoe found at Dumbuck crannog … Mr Adam Millar, F.S.A. was able to see it placed in

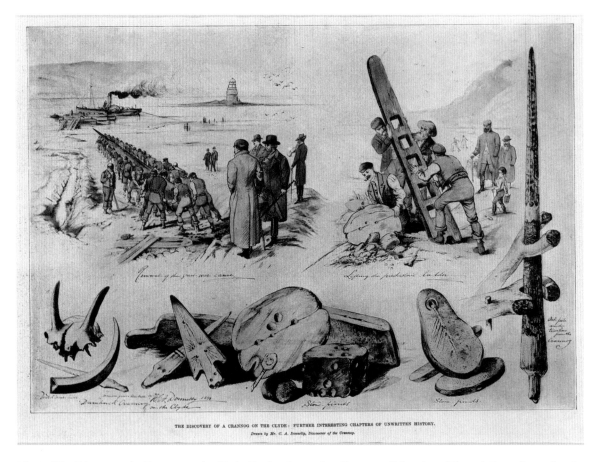

Fig. 31 'The Discovery of a Crannog on the Clyde: Further Interesting Chapters of Unwritten History'. Donnelly produced a colourful montage for the Illustrated London News, 19 November 1898. It shows the logboat being lifted by more than 30 men, the ladder and some of the small finds. (SC936013)

Mr Paton's custody at the Kelvingrove Museum, together with the ladder, by seven p.m.' (*Glasgow Herald*, 22 October 1898)

Mr Deas and the Clyde Trust were to continue to have a strong involvement with the excavation. At the request of the Society of Antiquaries of Scotland, they were commissioned to do a complete and accurate survey of the crannog (Fig. 32). The survey plan and section drawings survive and are part of the Clydeport-owned archive, which is held by RCAHMS. The original plan is marked by the surveyors' pin pricks, which are a result of the triangulation method employed. In addition to a complete plan, the Clyde Trust undertook to cut a section through the platform.

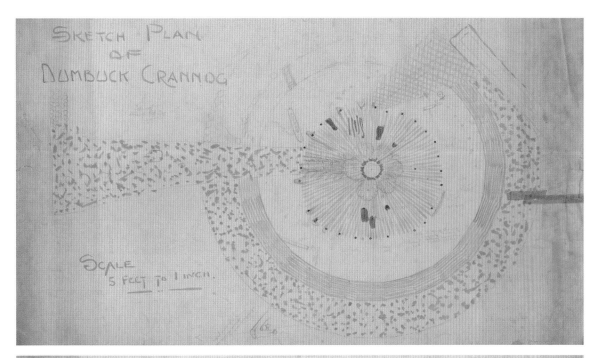

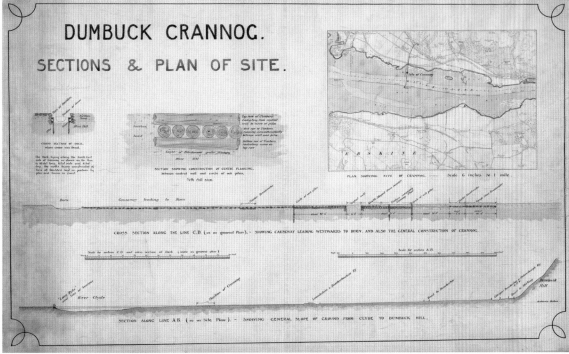

Fig. 32 The Clyde Trust plan and section. (SC004532 and SC004533)

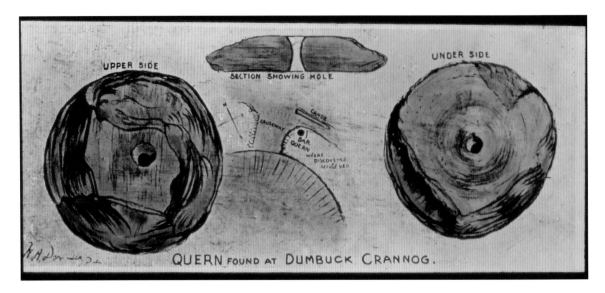

Fig. 33 'Quern Found at Dumbuck Crannog'. Donnelly's sketch of the quern stone and its location on the crannog. (SC709715)

The work of the Clyde Trust was captured by a contemporary journalist:

'At the crannog these June days the scene was very picturesque, the boats of the Clyde Trust riding, idly in the offing, while the sun-browned Clyde Trust men, so physically fit, toiled and laboured in the tropical sun, guided by Mr Mitchell and Mr Robertson. Many cuttings and sections were made, east, west, north and south. Mr Donnelly made it possible for them to do what has not hitherto been done - a section right into the crannog proper, wedge-shaped, in fact, a segment of the circular structure, revealing the fact so often recorded, that it is a timber structure not a stone one. Several valuable finds were made while prosecuting this work - some stone spear heads and also horn implements, large teeth, ribs, and chisels of horn. Mr. Robertson also unearthed a very formidable oaken war club four feet six inches [1.35m] long. The outstanding feature was revealed that the crannog was built on the secure foundation of a splendid bed of the finest blue clay. When Mr Deas has his plan and section made from very exhaustive measurements and levels it will form an independent and authoritative chart from which the actual position and levels of the crannog can be ascertained. The work was very trying in the waters and mud of the foreshore under a sun which recorded a temperature of 117 degrees in the light. Scientists all over the country are greatly indebted to Mr Deas for the sympathetic and practical manner he has approached this antiquarian work, and Mr Donnelly speaks in glowing terms of the efficient and practical manner in which the Clyde Trust men have executed the work on every occasion. Mr. Donnelly and his men, on behalf of the Helensburgh society have excavated 30,000 cubic feet of clay, sand and mud since first excavations were begun.' (Munro 1905, 172)

The Dumbuck finds

No pottery or metal finds were recorded during the excavations at Dumbuck and the overall tally of finds is relatively limited. Larger objects included the boat and ladder mentioned above, a cup-and-ring marked stone and part of a quern stone:

'Oct. 31st. One of the latest finds is a very fine quern, or millstone. The driving bar, of oak, 36 ins. [0.9m] long and about 3 ins. [76mm] wide, and ¹/₂ in. [12mm] thick, was found alongside, but in excavation it was broken into three or four pieces. The quern lay on a bed of refuse, which appears to be calcined acorns; ground and unground; the quern was got 21ft. [6.3m] outside the crannog proper, to the east of the causeway.' (Donnelly 1898b, 367)

A great deal of bone and horn was also uncovered:

'The remains of animals found, so far as they have been identified, are bones of the ox, horse, sheep or goat, swine, horns of the red deer and roe deer, and bones of a few large birds. The bones are mostly the long bones of the limbs, and are broken and splintered longitudinally, and many of them made into implements more or less sharpened at the points. One large pair of antlers of the red deer with part of the skull attached was found. One branch is complete and shows six tines, the other is partly broken. From tip to tip it must, when entire, have measured 48 inches [1.2m].' (Bruce 1900, 440)

Despite the rather poor range of finds, the Dumbuck material was remarkable in one respect, the discovery of a series of at least 30 unusual objects made of stone and shell.

Fig. 34 'First Image of Shale Discovered in the Refuse of the Relic Bed, of the Dumbuck Crannog by Rev. George Lamb' 1898. (SC709721)

Fig. 35 'Smallest Shale Image From Dumbuck Crannog Found in Excavating Debris in Well-Like Cavity in the Centre'. (SC709725)

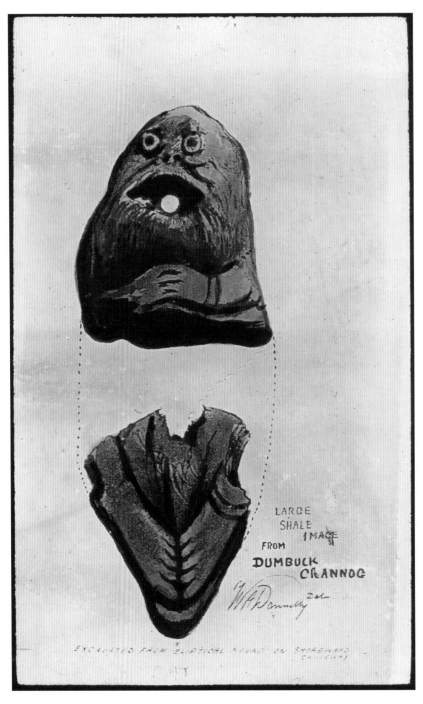

LARGE
SHALE
IMAGE
FROM
DUMBUCK
CRANNOG

EXCAVATED FROM ELIPTICAL MOUND ON SHOREWARD CAUSEWAY

Fig. 36 'Large Shale Image From Dumbuck Crannog'. This object is perhaps carved to represent Donnelly. (SC709724)

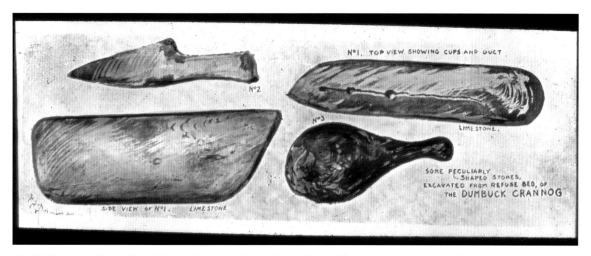

Fig. 37 'Some Peculiarly Shaped Stones Excavated From Refuse Bed, of the Dumbuck Crannog'. (SC709716)

They comprise one of the most unusual collections of small finds from any archaeological site in Scotland. The surfaces of these objects are carved with lines, circles or representations of human faces and bodies. The objects resemble those found during previous excavations at Dumbowie dun (Millar 1896). It was these objects rather than the crannog itself that caused most press speculation and controversy. From press cuttings and articles it is clear that these objects were found by a variety of individuals. This fact would come to be important once the controversy surrounding these artefacts began. Bruce is credited as having found a slate spearhead, 'about amidships' in the logboat (Donnelly 1898a, 285). Bruce excavated the deposits within the logboat, claiming the discovery of a number of objects:

'It was at once cleared out inside by myself, and in the bottom were found a spear-shaped slate object, similar to others found about the structure, an ornamented oyster shell, which has since mouldered away, a stone pendant ornament, and an implement of bone.' (Bruce 1900, 439)

Fig. 38 A public visit to Dumbuck. (SC709731)

Bruce was not the only one working on the logboat and it is noted that Donnelly also uncovered a much decayed *'arrowhead of bone'* embedded in the deposits at the bottom of the bow end. Unusual objects were also recovered from the central pit, such as an oyster shell with an unusual line-and-dot motif, also recovered by Bruce.

Many of these objects appear in Donnelly's illustrations, in some case annotated with the location of the discovery and the name of the finder (Fig. 34). For example, a small figurine is marked as having been found by the Rev George Lamb, though in a letter to the editor of the *Glasgow Herald*, Donnelly identifies the finder as the Rev George Lang:

'The "idol" was not "picked up from the mud in the canoe", it was excavated from the bottom of the refuse bed by the Rev George Lang, a gentleman to whose careful excavation and powers of observation much credit is due. As to his exercise of these qualifications archaeology is

Fig. 39 Visitors to the crannog inspect some of the excavations. (SC709730)

indebted for quite a number of valuable finds. The rev. gentleman's idea is that he fractured the object with his spade, as the two portions were found at different times.' (Glasgow Herald, 7 January 1899)

Elsewhere Donnelly comments on the character of some of the figurines (Fig. 35):

'The type is not by any means repulsive, but the mouth opened wide, and the cavity being a perforation right through, gives it a decidedly comical and somewhat lifelike expression in some lights; the workmanship is not artistic, it is of primitive and rude fashioning, but nevertheless graphic. It was picked out of the loam and sand in the central part of the structure.'
(Donnelly 1898b, 370)

In addition to these anthropomorphic figurines, a number of stone objects were found, which included a possible cup-marked stone (Fig. 37).

Fig. 40 A crowd gathers around Donnelly as he shows some of the small finds. (SC709732)

Public interest and site visits

The investigations generated a great deal of public interest and led to visits by several learned societies while the work was being carried out. It is clear, however, that some visits to the site had a less than benign purpose:

'It is painful to have to state that some visitors a short time ago used levers to prize asunder pieces of the canoe, especially on the bow end, and carried the plunder away. This and the disturbing of some of the larger beams of the crannog structure is most regrettable. When the public understand that the ladies and gentlemen of the Helensburgh Society are doing this work in the interest of science and that the results in experience and the finds are pro bono publico. They may take thought and do all in their power to aid the society. Chief Constable McHardy, who is a member of the society has given instructions that his men are to use those powers which Act of Parliament confer dealing with

antiquities being now discovered, as well as ancient monuments worthy of record or preservation … the crannog has been enclosed within a stake and wire fence and a notice put up requesting the public to refrain from interfering with the structure.' (*Evening Times*, 14 October 1898)

The visit of at least one society is recorded in a contemporary photograph (Fig. 38), and though undated the 'keep out' sign referred to in the *Evening Times* on 14 October 1898 is clearly visible. The central figure in the photograph, in the light suit, is Munro, who visited the site on Wednesday, 12 October, in the company of the Glasgow Archaeological Society. Donnelly can be seen on the far right of the image. Munro describes the visit from alighting the train at Bowling station where:

'Mr. Donnelly was waiting for us, and after getting ourselves rigged out in big boots we made our way, ankle-deep in mud, to the crannog. Here we inspected the canoe, a heavy oak beam with four or five ladder-like steps cut out of the solid, the remains of a kitchen midden containing ashes and quantities of broken bones, and a circular area paved with prepared timbers, some of which bore the marks of a metal axe. I was very anxious to see the rest of the relics, as I had heard of a barbed harpoon being among them, so Mr. Donnelly very kindly sent one of his men to fetch them. These I looked over carefully. Among the stone objects (excepting the precious objects in the case) I could not say with any certainty that any of them had been fashioned by the hand of man, or showed any signs of having been used as implements.' (Munro 1905, 155-6)

Fig. 41 '"Doing" the Crannog'. (SC709705, SC709704)

In another photograph, which has been hand-coloured, a group can be seen visiting the excavations (Fig. 39). Donnelly can be seen towering above them to the right of the image. The gentleman with the bowler hat in the foreground has his feet either side of the curving trench that followed the excavation of the refuse bed. This is probably the figure of Chief Constable Charles McHardy, who was able to use his position to protect the site after the incident of vandalism reported in the *Evening Times*. McHardy, became Chief Constable of the Dumbartonshire Constabulary in 1884. He was known for carving walking sticks and delicate ivory brooches with a pocket knife, at one point carving a walking stick by Royal Command for Queen Victoria (Duff 1998).

On these occasions the finds from the excavation were shown off to visitors by Bruce, Donnelly or Millar. In one of the photographs Donnelly can be seen holding court to an expectant crowd. In the background to the right a table is laid out with further finds (Fig. 40). The location of this photograph is the access under the railway 600m to the north-west of the crannog. Such visits are described in some of the press cuttings:

'The interest in the crannog on the Clyde still continues. The Glasgow Geological Society paid an official excursion to it on Saturday, guided by the discoverer, Mr W A Donnelly, artist, Milton, Bowling. The satisfaction and pleasure derived from the visit was effectively expressed by the secretary, Mr John Renwick, in moving a vote of thanks to Mr Donnelly, a vote warmly carried by the assembled members present, nearly 100. Mr Donnelly suitably replied. The Alexandria Natural History Society also visited the cranog, headed by their president, the Rev Mr Millar. The visitors had the features of the find explained to them, and were shown a large number of the productions of the refuse mud. The day was stormy and wet, and gave an idea of the difficulties which the excavators have to contend with in wind and weather, besides the tide. The Natural History Society of Glasgow and the Philosophical Society will visit the crannog on an early date.' (Evening Times, 20 October 1898)

Donnelly also recorded several of the visitors in his pictures. In *'"Doing"the Crannog'* (Fig. 41) a finely-attired woman in late 19th-century dress is shown. A well-dressed gentleman also appears in the collection, his rolled up trousers the only concession to the wet and muddy state of the foreshore. These images may be Donnelly's attempt to cast the banks of the Clyde in a more appealing light and to broaden the interest in the excavations. These two people have not been identified, but another of the pictures (Fig. 42) shows Munro and Anderson peering into the trench.

Fig. 42 Munro and Anderson inspect one of the trenches. (SC709702)

ARGUMENT, DISPUTE AND DISAGREEMENT

A controversy emerges: 1898-1899

By mid-October 1898 excavations at Dumbuck crannog had been underway for about a month and had already drawn considerable interest from both learned societies and the general public. Visits to the site were frequent and often reported in the local press. One visit, however, on Wednesday, 12 October 1898, was to spark a debate that would run for years. Amongst the people visiting the site was Dr Robert Munro, who had initially encouraged Donnelly to undertake excavation (Fig. 42). In summing up his visit, Munro complimented the excavators on their work, but cast considerable doubt over the genuineness of the finds:

'As for the stone weapons and the other relics in the case I ignored them altogether, stating that, in my opinion, they were not productions of the people who constructed and inhabited this strange place.' (*Glasgow Herald,* 7 January 1899)

Donnelly was clearly troubled by Munro's doubts and made reference to them in his correspondence with the *Journal of the British Archaeological Association*:

'The work still proceeds with satisfactory results, and is viewed with mixed feelings by some, but the majority rejoice that such an opportunity has arisen to study this page in the life of Pre-historic Man.' (Donnelly 1898b, 364)

Privately, Adam Millar wrote to Munro the day after his visit, on 13 October stating how unhappy Donnelly was that Munro should have cast doubt on some of the finds. Munro was quick to reply:

'Dear Mr Millar,   13th October 1898
Thanks for your letter. I returned home deeply impressed with the importance of your Clyde crannog and the novel character of the structures revealed. Nothing could be more satisfactory than the care bestowed on the investigation by Mr Donnelly, everything being carried out with skill and care; and I hope his services will be ultimately rewarded by something more substantial than mere archaeological fame. I lay much value on the bones recovered, and I trust you will lose no time in putting them into the hands of Professor Cleland, of Glasgow University.
At the same time, I did not think it right to reserve to myself the impression that some of the objects shown to me – the great spearhead, the image and pendant, and perhaps, one or two more of the objects – were products of the 19th century. My present opinion is that there is some mystification going on which it would be in the interest of archaeology as well as those conducting the investigations to clear up.
What the object may be, whether as a joke or for the satisfaction of bewildering so-called experts, I know not.

Fig. 43 Donnelly and other excavators on Dumbuck. (SC709701)

The matter lies in the hands of Mr Bruce and Mr Donnelly for further elucidation, and all I have to say is that if these objects are brought forward before the archaeological world as relics from the crannog you will be subject to as much criticism as M. de Rougemont.

If you are all satisfied as to their genuineness, of course I have nothing more to say in the meantime. Mr Donnelly is quite right in keeping everything for examination, but I could not pretend to be a friend of his without giving him the benefit of my impressions.

I have read his notice in the 'Illustrated News' and there is nothing wrong about it.

When I return I will be happy to join with you in consultation over the whole matter before you give further publicity to some of the finds. The crannog is sufficiently important without such extras.

Believe me, yours faithfully,
Robert Munro'
(*Glasgow Herald*, 16 January 1899).

Louis de Rougemont (1847-1921) claimed to be an explorer, and also impersonated a doctor, a photographer and an inventor. He published his adventures, which led to many readers questioning their veracity in the *Daily Chronicle*. In 1898 his impersonations caught up with him and he was exposed as a fraud.

A chance meeting with Bruce at Lanark Station a few days later prompted Munro to take the issue further, writing to him on 16 October 1898 and urging him to set up a committee of enquiry. Bruce's reply rejected the notion of an enquiry (18 October 1898) and in doing so reaffirmed the growing division between Munro and the excavators:

'I had a talk yesterday when in Edinburgh with Dr. Anderson, and agreed to let matters remain at present in status quo.' (Munro 1905, 157)

By November 1898, relations between Munro and the excavators had deteriorated still further, following a note that appeared in *Natural Science* that both misquoted Munro and publicly associated him with the progress of the Dumbuck excavation and its finds. This article prompted Munro to write his own piece for the *Glasgow Herald*, printed on Saturday, 7 January 1899, in which he publicly disassociated himself from the comments made in the *Natural Science* article. Munro's article is an extremely important resource in the investigation of the controversy surrounding Dumbuck. At the time it acted as the catalyst to many years of public controversy, but today it also provides insight into the thinking of the key players. In parallel with criticisms of the press today, Munro was evidently incensed that the journalist had misquoted him:

'It is somewhat singular that casual expressions which may have fallen from me with regard to the novelty and peculiarity of that structure should have been collected and published as a quotation, while not a syllable of remarks made at the same time on another phase of the investigation, and which were anything but complimentary, should have been altogether omitted.' (Munro 1905, 153)

Munro was keen to stress that similar strange objects had also been found at Dumbowie by the Helensburgh Society in 1895 (Millar 1896). Munro noted, perhaps with a hint of sarcasm, that the finds from both sites were not just the work of the same civilization but also the product of the same artist. He was tacitly accusing someone on the team of excavators of forgery, and his conclusion stated more strongly than ever his position on the matter:

'In attempting to solve the riddle of this most remarkable art gallery – idols, amulets and ornaments of shale and shell – there are just two alternative conclusions to be formulated. Either these objects are what the investigators assert them to be – the genuine relics of the inhabitants of the fort and crannog, or they are not. On the former hypothesis we have before us the most remarkable collection of archaeological remains ever found in Scotland. On the latter, they are the productions of some idle practical joker.' (Munro 1905, 159)

The reaction of the excavators to Munro's challenges is neatly captured in a letter from Millar to the *Glasgow Herald*, written on 13 January and published on the following Monday, 16 January 1899:

'Sir, - Doctor Munro's contribution to your paper on Saturday last is a very extraordinary article in more senses than one. As my name is involved in his insinuations and charges, I beg you will find space for this letter…. The committee of the Helensburgh Society has had to change its plans by reasons of Dr Munro's article. It has stopped all further digging. The planks laid down for the comfort of visitors are to be removed, the stepping-stone laid down by us also removed, and I am to write to the secretaries of the parent society in Edinburgh to endeavour to get them to make such examination as they may see fit in the parts of the crannog which so far are untouched by us. Dr Munro did not write in any official capacity, so far as I can judge, but in an individual capacity, and I hope the council of Society of Antiquaries of Scotland will not approve of his action in this matter. I have now to beg that Dr Munro will produce reasons to justify the insinuation he has made in respect of the productions from Dunbuie and from the crannog. He will readily see that though he was dealing with a few stones he was also dealing with the reputation of honest men, who are also careful antiquarians – I am, etc., ADAM MILLAR' (*Glasgow Herald*, 13 January 1899).

Donnelly also replied to Munro's article, though this appears to be his only contribution to the ensuing debate until 1902. In his reply Donnelly was keen to point out his position:

'Personally I wish to state that, as the discoverer of what my learned friends are good enough to call "a valuable addition to the archaeology of the century," I do not, therefore, put myself forth as an authority. I have never done so. I have tried as an artist, not as an antiquary, to give a faithful

Fig. 44 William Donnelly surrounded by workers and helpers, with some of the small finds at his feet. (SC709733)

record of all I saw with both pen and pencil, to protect at all costs the discovery and finds from destruction' (*Glasgow Herald*, January 1899).

During the ensuing months the debate gathered pace with tens of thousands of words being written in letters to the editors of the *Evening Times* and the *Glasgow Herald*. Numerous people expounded their theories and declared their support for one camp or the other. Sometimes the correspondents were prepared to use their names, notable examples being Andrew Lang, poet and novelist, and the Reverend Robert Munro, not to be confused with the Dr Robert Munro. In addition to the named authors, many people used cryptic pseudonyms such as 'High Water', 'XYZ', 'Delta' and 'Far West', perhaps because the debate had become so vitriolic. In these letters the passion and curiosity of the authors is clear to all.

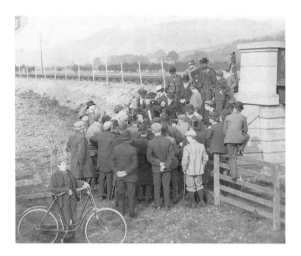

Fig. 45 William Donnelly discussing the crannog with a learned audience on Wednesday, 12 October 1898. (SC961083)

The controversy comes to a head: 1900-1905

The death of Adam Millar in 1900 heralded the loss of one of the key Dumbuck supporters and one of the original directors of the excavation. It is also in this year that a paper by Bruce appeared in the *Proceedings of the Society of Antiquaries of Scotland*, detailing both the excavation at Dumbuck and the finds uncovered. As a result of the controversy surrounding the site the Society made the unprecedented step of also publishing the comments of members present at the meeting during which the paper was read. In summing up, the Chairman, Sir Arthur Mitchell, reflected on the widely divergent opinions of the members and attempted to draw a diplomatic veil over the controversy:

'The comments which have been made on Mr Bruce's paper will, I think, serve a useful purpose. The fact that they have by no means been all in agreement does not, in my opinion, lessen their value. It seems to me that the position of the Society as a corporate body has already been on the whole satisfactorily disclosed in regard to the question, or rather the doubts which have largely led to these comments. But a little more may perhaps with advantage be said. The Society as a whole—that is in its corporate capacity—has no function or duty to give a deliverance on such a matter; but, of course, the individual Fellows composing the Society may hold opinions which differ, and differ greatly. The Society, indeed, cannot put an end to such differences by any deliverance. It could not do so even if it wished.' (Bruce 1900, 460)

Whether as a result of this paper or simply because the topic had seemed to run its course, there was little correspondence in the papers concerning Dumbuck during 1901 and 1902. Shortly after the Dumbuck excavations another crannog in the Clyde was investigated, this time on the south shore, near Langbank (Fig. 7, Langbank East; Bruce 1908). John Bruce led the investigations under the auspices of a committee appointed by the Glasgow Archaeological Society. The archaeological authorities of the time were evidently guarding against a repeat of the Dumbuck events, and the committee published a signed report which was at pains to state that the workmen employed on-site, all of whom were Clyde Trust staff, had *'not been associated with previous explorations'* (Bruce 1908, 52) and therefore were not connected with the forgeries. However, the report also states that the Clyde Trust workmen were only involved in the second season of excavations, in the Autumn of 1902. Preliminary work had taken place the year before, and it was perhaps in this first season of work, in October 1901, that four shale objects like those from Dumbuck were uncovered (Bruce 1908, nos 5-8). The Dumbuck issue reappeared again in 1903, with the publication of a letter in the *Glasgow Herald* entitled 'Crannog or Fish Bothy?'. The letter was written by Rev Robert Munro, a regular contributor to the original debate and a supporter of Dr Robert Munro's position on the topic. Rev Munro's opening statement sets the tone of the ensuing debate:

'In 1898 a curious wooden structure, with outer layers of piles, was found on the margin of the river Clyde, near Dumbuck. Its discoverers at once called it a Crannog; and since then they not only stuck to the name but they have, by pen and pencil, and in every possible way, sought to magnify its importance and extend its reputation.' (*Glasgow Herald*, 28 March 1903)

This letter sparked a flurry of replies and, if anything, the sentiment became more intense than that expressed during the original exchanges. The replies were published together in the *Glasgow Herald* on 15 May 1903. A regular correspondent, during this period, was Reverend Mr H J Dukinfield Astley; one of his letters in particular demonstrates how acrimonious the debate became:

'Sir, as the Rev. R. Munro, M.A. D.D., of Old Kilpatrick has thought it necessary to devote so much of his (presumably) valuable time and to

take up more than a column of your valuable space, I will not say in controverting the arguments of his opponents, but in personal ridicule and abuse, I think it incumbent upon me to take some notice of his letter. My reply will be brief, because I shall not attempt to emulate the peculiar methods of controversy indulged in by your correspondent, nor to repeat what I have already said in your columns and elsewhere. Before passing on, however, I would remark that it certainly seems a pity that Mr. Munro is not a member of a communion in which he might find full scope for his talents, because in his own opinion, at anyrate, he has all the qualifications to render him eligible for the office of infallible Pope!' (*Glasgow Herald*, 15 May 1903)

William Donnelly kept a close eye on the emerging discussion and contributed regularly to the newspaper over the next few months. However, perhaps one of the most telling pieces of evidence of his own state of mind is to be found in private correspondence to Ludovic McLellan Mann. In this letter dated 26 July 1903, Donnelly both refers to Astley's stinging attack and possibly also reveals how personally affected he was by the ongoing controversy:

'Dear Mr Mann,
How pleased I was to see you occupying such a prominent position in the report in the "Herald" of your first find.
Pray accept my warmest congratulations, till I call on you. I have called several times but I was not in luck. I would like the favour of drawing a few sketches of some of your finds.
THAT IS if ANY outsider is going to do so. But your pleasure.

Remembering what you said to me - regarding
your alden time friend Dr. David Murray. I had
the pleasure to give a warm response to a very
polite and courteous note from him desiring that I
should assist & guide his FRIEND Mr. Hamilton
C.E. (a specialist & built [?] on scientific lines) he
came, he saw and he scored on the Crannog he
and two assistants "rods" "chains" [...] They did
not make it but a "fish bothy" I made them
welcome as all I desire is "Light more Light!"
Munro is lying low just the mine is only
smoldering Wasn't that a stinger that last of
Astley's how he went for him
your PERIOD still holds the field
Yours very truly
W.A. Donnelly.'
(RCAHMS, MS/678/35/33)

Further letters continued to be written through
1903 and 1904, but the controversy reached a
peak in June 1905, with the publication of
Munro's book *Archaeology and False Antiquities*
(Munro 1905). In this he outlined the
controversy and clarified that in his view the
crannog was genuine. The objects however, or
as he preferred to call them *'the false
antiquities'*, were plainly not genuine
antiquities. In December of the same year
Donnelly died, an event that his son Gerald
subsequently placed in part on the shoulders
of those who doubted the veracity of the
Dumbuck finds:

*'From the time of the discovery of the crannog and
my father's death in December, 1905, the
controversy was particularly acute, and indeed
this unfortunate matter was one of the causes
which contributed to his comparatively early
death.'* (*Evening Times*, 21 October 1932)

Gerald Donnelly's view is supported by a
typescript of his father's held in the RCAHMS
archives. It is uncertain where Donnelly
intended to present this work, but Munro's book
in particular was evidently causing him concern:

*'This book with the suggestive title of "Archaeology
and False Antiquities", as a matter of fact deals
with the Dumbuck Crannog from beginning to end
of its 400 pages. To support his original captious
and dogmatically hypercritical theories he has
dragged in object lessons and authorities from the
four winds of Heaven, but the greater part of his
so-called proofs are from the seamy and shady side
of human nature, of which the Learned Doctor
seems to possess quite an exceptional insight,
claiming for himself the self-elected position of
both Judge and Jury'* (RCAHMS, MS/678/35/10).

The manuscript goes on to suggest that in this
instance Munro was both ignorant and biased,
and shows that Donnelly felt persecuted by
Munro's writings and the victim of his *'most
poisoned darts'*. It is at this stage that Donnelly
clearly demonstrates how much the whole
sorry business had taken out of him:

*'All the same I still survive with sufficient vitality
to prove to my friends and supporters that my
contentions are worthy of their sympathetic
consideration and also that Dr. Munro may have
an opportunity of knowing that he is not
infallible, for infallibility seems to be his strongest
point.'*(RCAHMS, MS/678/35/10)

After the publication of Munro's book and
William Donnelly's untimely death, the
Dumbuck controversy seems to have faded
from view until the 1930s.

The controversy re-emerges: 1932

In 1932 the status of the Clyde objects was once again thrown into the public domain. A French book by Vayson de Pradenne, Professor at the Ecole d'Anthropologie, Paris, was published in March. In it he reiterated Munro's view that most of the finds were modern fabrications. In reviewing this book, Vere Gordon Childe, Abercromby Professor of Archaeology at the University of Edinburgh, also passed comment on Dumbuck:

'the only extensive fraud in this country which has had any lasting repercussions is that of Dumbuck and Dumbowie which Munro exposed with ruthless directness.' (Childe 1932, 472)

Not everyone accepted this judgment, and Ludovic Mann was quick to re-enter the fray. He claimed the existence of a newly discovered 'metric test', to which he had submitted all the Dumbuck finds. The system of measurement contained *'the twin prehistoric units of 0.619 inch and 0.553 inch'* (*The Scotsman*, 27 April 1932). He concluded that:

'the so-called Clyde forgeries of 1898, not only in their dimensions but in their incised design, enshrine the method of combining the twin measures in a single relic … no faker of 1898 could possibly have known of these intricate matters, and thus the relics supposed by some to be forgeries must be genuine.' (*Glasgow Herald*, 27 April 1932)

As we have seen, Mann had been a correspondent of Donnelly's and there is little doubt in which camp his sympathies lay.

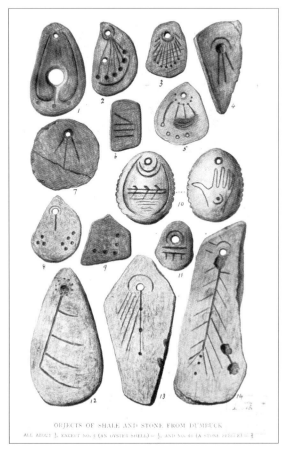

OBJECTS OF SHALE AND STONE FROM DUMBUCK
ALL ABOUT ⅓, EXCEPT NO. 5 (AN OYSTER SHELL) = ½, AND No. 10 (A STONE PEBBLE) = ¾

Fig. 46 'Objects of Shale and Stone From Dumbuck.' An illustration taken from Munro's book Archaeology and False Antiquities.

For Gerald Donnelly this was an all-important discovery, and in his view vindicated his father and restored his reputation. However, the 'metric test' did not find favour with contemporary archaeologists and has long since sunk from view.

DUMBUCK IN THE 21ST CENTURY

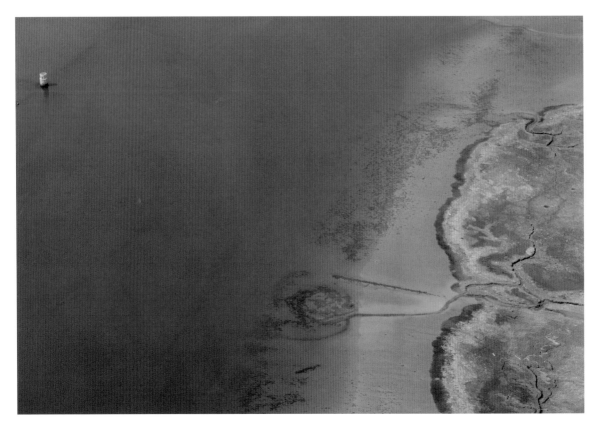

Fig. 47 Dumbuck today. (SC970227)

Recent research

In 1998 work began anew, 100 years on from the original excavation (Sands and Hale 2001). In the course of this work, which was funded by Historic Scotland, the crannog was re-surveyed and a small trench was excavated. The aims of the project were to understand what still survives, and to verify a number of questions that have arisen from research into the results of the original excavation (Sands, Hale and Miller forthcoming).

In undertaking these excavations, in the same wet and muddy conditions as the original excavators, it was hard not to become curious about the people involved a century earlier. Harder still, when another of the forgeries turned up in the excavation (Fig. 49). Work on the site also revealed traces of the previous excavators, including original posts erected to deter vandals and the remains of a bucket, perhaps carried by Ned or Dan.

The controversy today

The recovery of yet another of the forgeries in 2000, implies that there are more to be found and that the crannog was liberally salted. The object comprises a small, smooth piece of shale with carvings on one of the surfaces. The carvings are obviously not of any antiquity. Finally, the question arises as to who produced the fakes and planted them on the site, and why? William Donnelly undertook the excavations of both Dumbowie and Dumbuck in collaboration with professional archaeologists so that the sites could be rigorously investigated. What would he gain from planting the forgeries? His reputation might have been elevated as an archaeologist, and this might have enhanced the market for his articles and drawings in the popular press. Equally, he had as much to lose by exposure. In any case his distress in the face of the allegations seems to have been genuine, which would suggest that he is not implicated.

So, what of John Bruce, his co-director. He found similar objects on Langbank East, an excavation that Donnelly was not involved with, but he too appears deeply shocked. It fell to him to present the findings to the Society of Antiquaries of Scotland, despite the evident hostility in that quarter. Apparently he escaped the suspicion of his peers, and his career survived untainted. He became Vice-President of the Society of Antiquaries of Scotland in 1919, and published extensively on all manner of Scottish archaeology. Adam Millar, the third of the directors, died before the discovery of the forgeries on Langbank East and was surely not the perpetrator.

If Donnelly and Bruce are out of the frame our attention must turn to the other people involved with the excavation, to those who had access to the site and some artistic talent. Is it conceivable that a man such as Chief Constable McHardy, the carver of walking sticks, could have been involved? Surely a man in his position had far too much to lose. Some suspicion at the time was directed towards the paid excavators, but there is no evidence that they had anything to do with the fabrication of the objects. In truth we will probably never know. Perhaps the persons responsible had a grudge against the directors, the Helensburgh Society or the archaeological establishment of the time. Perhaps it was a practical joke that got out of hand. Certainly

Fig. 48 Excavating the excavators, perhaps this is the bucket carried by Ned or Dan?

their handiwork caused some impressive ructions in the professional and personal lives of those involved. All we can deduce is that the forger or forgers had an intimate knowledge of the crannog. Simply to place the objects without being detected implies first-hand knowledge of the site, the order in which the particular structures were to be excavated and an understanding of the tides.

Despite the controversy, the archive of the original excavation contains a remarkable record of the structures that were encountered all those years ago. By the same token,

CM

Fig. 49 The forgery discovered in 2000.

Donnelly's illustrations convey their character as vividly as any modern photograph or plan. Portions of the crannog are still relatively undisturbed, leaving us with an important structure that still has much to tell us about life on the Clyde some two thousand years ago. We are also left with a fascinating story about a group of people whose lives and reputations were scrutinised in the national press and academic journals alike at the turn of the 19th century. The enduring appeal of Dumbuck crannog is the fact that this mystery remains unsolved.

APPENDIX

Diary of events: 1898 - 1900

This section provides a brief chronological overview of the progress of the excavation and the emergence of the controversy.

Sunday, 31 July 1898	Discovery of crannog by Donnelly. 31 July is the date mentioned in the typescript numbered MS/678/35/10 in the RCAHMS archive. Tidal records would suggest that Donnelly observed the remains sometime in the afternoon.
Tuesday, 16 August	Munro's first visit to Dumbuck.
Thursday, 25 August	Shortly after Munro's visit Donnelly guided the excavation committee of the Helensburgh Society to the crannog. Although no date is recorded for this visit, the presence of a pre-excavation sketch provides a likely date (Fig. 21). It was after this visit that an extraordinary meeting of the Society was called and a decision made to undertake an excavation.
Tuesday, 20 September	The exact date upon which the excavation started is unknown, but one of the pictures shows it is well under way by September 20. This is also the date of the report sent by Donnelly to the *Journal of the British Archaeological Association* (Donnelly 1898a), which indicates that by this date the canoe had been found and partly excavated. It is also apparent that some of the controversial objects had been found.
Wednesday, 21 September	Structural details start to emerge (Fig. 12).
Thursday, 22 September	In addition to further excavations of the refuse bed (Fig. 27) and the surrounding structure, the discovery of the ladder is shown in a painting of this date (Fig. 30). This is later mentioned in an article in the *Evening Times* entitled: 'The Ancient Crannog in the Firth of Clyde – Further Interesting Discoveries' dated Thursday, 20 October 1898.
Friday, 23 September	'Dan and Ned, Constable Mr McHardy at the crannog. More finds of stone implements, scrapers borers and hammers' (Fig. 23).
Saturday, 24 September	Visit by the Glasgow Archaeological Society and the Helensburgh Society. *'Dan and Ned early down making ready for the Helensburgh Society and the Society of Archaeologists of Glasgow',* written in Donnelly's hand on the drawing dated Friday 23 September 1898 (Fig. 23).
Monday, 26 September	The drawing dated Friday, 23 September also includes some general sketches of the Clyde drawn on the 26 September. These show both shipping on the river and give the impression of stormy conditions (Fig. 23).
Wednesday, 5 October	On this date, or shortly before, the path leading from the platform towards the boat dock was revealed (Fig. 14).
Saturday, 8 October	Newspaper clipping entitled *'Another important find at the Dumbuck Crannog',* mentions the recent discovery of the cup-marked rock.

Monday, 10 October	An article in the *Evening Times*, dated 14 October 1898, entitled 'The Important Antiquarian Discovery on the Clyde', reported that *'The advancing tide of Monday caused the suspension of work, just as a fresh discovery was being made'*.
Wednesday, 12 October	Munro's second visit to Dumbuck and the start of the controversy. Letter received by Munro from Mr Adam Millar, saying *'his friend Donnelly was rather depressed by my suspicions as to the genuineness of some of the finds'*.
Thursday, 13 October	Munro replies to Millar's letter.
Friday, 14 October	Some time prior to this Friday, and probably Munro's visit on 12 October, the site was vandalized, prompting Chief Constable McHardy to erect a fence and a sign. During this week it was established that the logboat lay in a well constructed dock.
Saturday, 15 October	Visit by the Glasgow Geological Society.
Friday, 21 October	The removal of Dumbuck logboat was organised by Mr Deas, engineer-in-chief of the Clyde Trust, and conducted on site by Mr L McIntosh, river superintendent, with the assistance of Mr A M A Young and Mr J L Robertson. The logboat is in the custody of the Kelvingrove Museum, together with the ladder, by 7 pm.
Friday, 28 October	Further structural evidence is revealed (Fig. 29).
Saturday, 29 October	The exposure of the breakwater is mentioned in Donnelly's letters to the *Journal of the British Archaeological Association* (Donnelly 1898b, 367).
Monday, 31 October	A quern stone is found (Fig. 33).
Tuesday, 8 November	Painting showing structural details, looking from the ring of piles towards the centre of the crannog (Fig. 17).
Friday, 11 November	Stone circles uncovered (Fig. 6).
Wednesday, 16 November	Letter sent by Munro to Bruce urging him to appoint a committee of enquiry to explore the artefacts being found at Dumbuck crannog.
Thursday, 17 November	Bruce visited Edinburgh and met with Anderson. During their discussion they decided that no committee should be set up to look into the nature of the Dumbuck artefacts.
Friday, 18 November	Letter sent by Bruce to Munro rejecting the need for a committee of enquiry.
Wednesday, 23 November	Donnelly mentions the discovery of more *'weird little objects'* during the period between 31 October and 23 of November. He also mentions the start of the excavation of the central pit, which he had resisted excavating until he could *'watch every spadeful and every move, in case of damaging any fragile feature'* (Donnelly 1898b, 368).

Saturday, 7 January 1899	Key newspaper article in the *Glasgow Herald* by Munro entitled, 'Recent Archaeological Discoveries – The Crannog at Dumbuck', in which he outlines his position.
Monday, 16 January	First indication that excavations are to be drawn to a close as a result of the negative publicity.
Thursday, 19 January	Paper read by Donnelly to the Glasgow Archaeological Society. Dr David Murray, LL.D., president of the society was in the chair. Mr J Dalrymple Duncan, Hon. Secretary, was also present.
Saturday, 21 January	At a meeting of the Acting Committee of the Council of the Society of Antiquaries of Scotland, held within their Council Room, a letter was read *'from Mr Adam J Millar announcing the resolution of the Helensburgh Society to cease work at Dumbuck … the secretary was instructed to answer it'*. There was a visit to the crannog by the Andersonian Society of Glasgow.
Tuesday, 14 March	Donnelly's plan was drawn (Fig. 11).
Wednesday, 15 March	Paper read to the British Archaeological Association by Donnelly concerning the prehistoric remains in the Clyde valley.
Saturday, 8 April	In the afternoon, a party of 150, consisting of members of the Geological and Philosophical Societies of Glasgow, visited Dumbuck.
Monday, 12 June	This is an approximate date for the start of work on the Clyde Trust plan of the crannog (Munro 1905, 171). Undertaken by Mr Deas with the help of Donnelly (Fig. 32).
Saturday, 21 October	Meeting of the Acting Committee of the Council of the Society of Antiquaries of Scotland held within their Council Room. A letter from Bruce was read *'inquiring whether this Society could see its way to complete the excavation of the pile structure at Dumbuck'*. The response was 'referred to the Council'.
Friday, 10 November	The Council direct their Secretary to reply to the letter by Bruce, declining to undertake the work proposed, and explaining their reason for refusing.
Monday, 14 May 1900	At a meeting of the Society of Antiquaries of Scotland held within the library at the National Museum of Antiquaries of Scotland, the following communication was read: *'Notes of the discovery and exploration of a pile-structure on the north bank of the Clyde east from Dumbarton Rock'* by Bruce. Sir Arthur Mitchell, K.C.B., M.D., LL.D., was in the chair. Munro was also present.

REFERENCES

Blundell, O 1909, Notices of the examination by means of a diving dress of the artificial island or crannog of Eilean Muireach in the south end of Loch Ness, *Proceedings of the Society of Antiquaries of Scotland*, 43 (1908-9), 159-64.

Bruce, J 1896, Notice of remarkable groups of archaic sculpturings in Dumbartonshire and Stirlingshire, *Proceedings of the Society of Antiquaries of Scotland*, 30 (1895-6), 205-9.

Bruce, J 1900, Notes of the discovery and exploration of a pile structure on the north bank of the River Clyde, east from Dumbarton Rock, *Proceedings of the Society of Antiquaries of Scotland*, 34 (1899-1900), 437-62.

Bruce, J 1908, Report and investigations upon the Langbank pile dwelling, *Transactions of the Glasgow Archaeological Society*, New Series, 5 (1908), 43-53.

Childe, V G 1932, Review of A Vayson de Pradenne, Les frauds en archéologie préhistorique avec quelques exemples de comparaison en archéologie générale et sciences naturelles, *Antiquaries Journal*, 12 (1932), 470-2.

Crone, A 2000, *The History of a Scottish lowland Crannog: Excavations at Buiston, Ayrshire 1989-90*, STAR Monograph 4.

Donnelly, W A 1898a, Discovery of a Crannog on the shore of the Clyde in Dumbarton, *Journal of the British Archaeological Association*, New Series, 5(1898), 282-9.

Donnelly, W A 1898b, Tidal Crannog at Dumbarton, *Journal of the British Archaeological Association*, New Series, 5 (1898), 364-74.

Donnelly, W A 1900, The mound dwellings of Auchingaich, *Journal of the British Archaeological Association,* New Series, 6 (1900), 363-7.

Duff, J 1998, The McHardy Boys, *The Scots Magazine*, August 1998.

Evening Times, Friday, 14 October 1898, 'The Important Antiquarian Discovery on the Clyde' anon.

Evening Times, Thursday, 20 October 1898, 'The Ancient Crannog in the Firth of Clyde Further Interesting Discoveries' anon.

Evening Times, Friday, 21 October 1932, 'The Dumbuck Crannog. Question of Authenticity' W Gerald Donnelly.

Glasgow Herald, Saturday, 22 October 1898, 'The Pre-Historic Canoe of the Crannog on the Clyde' anon.

Glasgow Herald, Saturday, 7 January 1899, 'Recent Archaeological Discoveries: The Crannog at Dumbuck' Dr Robert Munro.

Glasgow Herald, Monday, 16 January 1899, 'Recent Archaeological Discoveries. Dumbuck and Dunbuie. Mr Millar's reply to Dr Munro'.

Glasgow Herald, January 1899, 'Recent Archaeological Discoveries Dumbuck and Dumbuie Statement by Mr Donnelly'.

Glasgow Herald, Saturday, 28 March 1903, 'Crannog or Fish Bothy' R Munro BD., Old Kilpatrick.

Glasgow Herald, Friday, 15 May 1903, 'Crannog or Fish Bothy, Mr Astely on his Defence' H J Dunkinfield Astley.

Glasgow Herald, Wednesday, 27 April 1932, 'Prehistoric Measures' Ludovic McL Mann.

Hale, A G C 2000, Marine crannogs: previous work and recent surveys, *Proceedings of the Society of Antiquaries of Scotland*, 130 (2000), 537-58.

Hale, A G C 2004, *Scottish Marine Crannogs*, BAR 369, Oxford.

Illustrated London News, Saturday 8 October 1898, 'The Recent Discovery of a lake-dwelling on the Clyde: sketches of the excavation'.

Illustrated London News, Saturday 19 November 1898, 'The Discovery of a Crannog on the Clyde: Further Interesting Chapters of Unwritten History'.

Maxwell, J H 1939, A bronze age cemetery at Springhill farm, Baillieston, near Glasgow, *Transactions of the Glasgow Archaeological Society*, 9, part 3, 287-302.

Millar, A 1896, Notes of the discovery and exploration of a circular fort on Dumbowie hill, near Dumbarton, *Proceedings of the Society of Antiquaries of Scotland*, 30 (1895-6), 291-308.

Morrison, I 1985, *Landscape with Lake Dwellings The Crannogs of Scotland*, Edinburgh.

Mowat, R J C 1996, *The Logboats of Scotland*, Oxbow Monograph 68, Oxford.

Munro, R 1882, *Ancient Scottish Lake Dwellings or Crannogs*, Edinburgh.

Munro, R 1890, *The Lake Dwellings of Europe*, London.

Munro, R 1905, *Archaeology and false antiquities*, London.

O'Sullivan, A 1998, *The Archaeology of Lake Settlement in Ireland*, Discovery Programme Monographs 4.

Ritchie, J N G 2002, Excavation archives: preservation and chance in the shadow of the Brochs, in Ballin Smith, B, and Banks, I (eds) (2002) *In the Shadow of the Brochs*, 205-16, Stroud.

Sands, R, and Hale, A 2001, Evidence from marine crannogs of later prehistoric use of the Firth of Clyde, *Journal of Wetland Archaeology*, 1 (2001), 41-54.

Sands, R, Hale, A G C and Miller, J forthcoming, Palaeoenvironmental evidence from Dumbuck crannog, Firth of Clyde.

Stuart, J 1866, Notices of a group of artificial islands in the Loch of Dowalton, Wigtonshire, and of other artificial islands or 'crannogs' throughout Scotland, *Proceedings of the Society of Antiquaries of Scotland*, 6 (1864-6), 114-78.

The Scotsman, 27 April 1932, 'Scottish Crannogs' Ludovic McL Mann.

Wood-Martin, W G 1886, *The lake-dwellings of Ireland or ancient lacustrine habitations of Erin commonly called crannogs*, Dublin.